Pattern Sourcebook:
Japanese Style
250 Patterns for Projects and Designs

Shigeki Nakamura

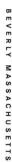

BEVERLY MASSACHUSETTS

ROCKPORT

PUBLISHERS

First published in the United States of America by
Rockport Publishers, a member of
Quayside Publishing Group
100 Cummings Center
Suite 406-L
Beverly, Massachusetts 01915-6101
Telephone: (978) 282-9590
Fax: (978) 283-2742
www.rockpub.com

ISBN-13: 978-1-59253-498-2
ISBN-10: 1-59253-498-8

10 9 8 7 6 5 4 3

Printed in Singapore

Preface

Japan has a long heritage of traditional colors, characters, and decorative designs, which have been passed down through the ages. This book focuses on decorative designs, providing a collection of materials and accompanying documentation for approximately 60 categories and 250 examples of Japanese designs that today's designers consider essential.

All of the images introduced in this book have been selected from among the stock of designs I have traced over the long years of my career, and they have been saved as JPEG and PSD files on the accompanying CD-ROM. The PSD-formatted files can be manipulated to modify the colors, textures, etc. of the background and foreground layers of each design using the functions of Adobe Photoshop, thus giving birth to original pieces and unlimited variation.

The commentary provided for the designs also includes a description of their histories and origins, uses, characteristics, and more. I hope that this book will be used widely as a practical Japanese-design production tool.

Shigeki Nakamura (Cobble collaboration)

Contents

*The patterns preceded by a small black circle (•) at the end of each chapter are examples specially selected by the author

How to use this book

[Explanatory Notes]

● This book is an illustrated compilation of existing traditional designs and focuses on specific themes. The name of each illustration represents the abbreviated name of the item followed by the name of the theme, (For example, "Primrose on short-sleeved Yuzen print kimono [*Yuzen-kosode Sakuraso*]")

● The purpose of the illustrations is to observe the origins of form from an evolutionary perspective. Divergent size, color, lines, etc. are not intended to express the original form of an actual item.

● While designs are digitally reproduced as true to the original work as possible, some illustrations have been modified using colors selected to ensure the least possible sense of discomfort in order to emphasize the theme.

● The chapters on plants were divided in this fashion not to represent the seasons at the time that the original designs were established, but in accordance with our modern aesthetic sense of seasons. Here, many of the winter plants are treated as representations of the coming of spring or spring plants in traditional patterns. Furthermore, since pine and bamboo are perennial plants, they have been classified in the winter grouping of pine, bamboo, and plum, which represent the festive "welcoming of spring."

● While the files on the accompanying CR-ROM generally describe single units of complete samples, layout of the images in this book may have required trimming and partial modification of colors.

● The images that relate to *komon* (literally, "small pattern"), such as *kimono*, which is among those recorded on the accompanying CD-ROM, may be interlinked on all sides, left to right, top to bottom.

Page Layout

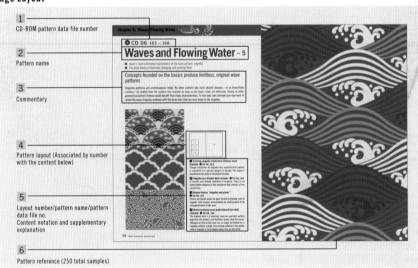

1 — CD-ROM pattern data file number

2 — Pattern name

3 — Commentary

4 — Pattern layout (Associated by number with the content below)

5 — Layout number/pattern name/pattern data file no.
Content notation and supplementary explanation

6 — Pattern reference (250 total samples)

Chapter 1
Plants/Spring

● CD 01 001 – 004

Spring Grasses

- The warmth of spring sunlight
- A breath of spring and the joy of life

The flowering grasses of spring are reminiscent of the gentleness of "hiragana" characters

While this chapter deals largely with the royal family of spring flowers—cherry blossoms, wisteria and peony—the flowering grasses found in the fields of spring are also brightly and effectively rendered in abundance. The flowering grasses of spring are not used as flower patterns as often as those of autumn, perhaps because they are considered lyrically inferior. In fact, while "the seven grasses of autumn [aki no nana-kusa]" were selected for the beauty of their flowers, by contrast, "the seven grasses of spring [haru no nana-kusa]" are treated as "vegetables."

1	4
2	
3	

1 Dandelions rendered in Nabeshima underglaze
● CD 01_001
While somewhat flamboyant, the rendering of leaves replete with a richness that is characteristic of Japanese expression serves as a good reference for form.

2 Crabapple rendered in Nabeshima underglaze
● CD 01_002
A well-balanced rendition of a luxuriant growth of flowers and leaves that at the same time successfully avoids a heaviness of expression.

3 Horsetails against brown in a short-sleeved Yuzen print kimono
● CD 01_003
This rendition can be considered a good example of simplicity compensated for by the seductiveness of the linear subject matter.

4 Primrose on a short-sleeved Yuzen print kimono
● CD 01_004
Though a seemingly typical rendition of form, the beauty of the flowers is complemented by the expression and pigmentation of the leaves.

⊙ CD 01 005 – 008
Cherry Blossoms – 1

■ Decorative patterns that do not suggest contrivance
■ Cherry blossoms firmly established as being representative of the "spirit" of Japan

A signature Japanese pattern that continues to command the adoration the Japanese people

Numerous cherry blossom patterns have been designed since about the time that the cherry blossom became more popular than the flowers of the plum tree as the theme of poems. Florid and most beautiful just before they fall, how fitting the cherry blossom must have seemed in the hearts and minds of the Japanese people. From innumerable varieties of flowers to broken branches, recreation, and so on, the cherry blossom pattern has evolved magnificently by incorporating the diverse factors that influence these flowers.

1	
2	4
3	

1 Cherry blossom pattern on a long-sleeved Yuzen print kimono ⊙ CD 01_005
The realistic nature of its expression aside, this is more effective as an example of pattern as design than as an example of painting.

2 Broken branch of a cherry tree rendered on an unlined kimono ⊙ CD 01_006
This rendition of a broken branch and lilting petals evokes for the viewer the image of cherry blossoms in full bloom.

3 Cherry blossom pattern rendered on a Chinese-style brocade kimono ⊙ CD 01_007
One's attention is drawn to the alignment of these changing double-flowering cherry blossoms where five-petal formations lay atop eight-petal formations in a fashion reminiscent of an armorial crest.

4 Cherry blossom pattern rendered on a decorative collar ⊙ CD 01_008
A lesson in the rendition of form and pigmentation of the odiferous sensuality of the cherry blossom.

⊙ CD 01 009 – 012
Cherry Blossoms – 2

- The many fruits of highly advanced realism of expression in design
- The aesthetic differences between the cherry blossom in nature and the cherry blossom rendered in design patterns

The changable design of the charm of natural beauty

The cherry blossom, resplendent in natural beauty. It is often said that no other flower exists whose beauty is as difficult to render true-to-life in paintings as the cherry blossom. This is one of the limitations of realistic expression. In the case of decorative patterns, designs are created to rid the observer of the "real view", and implements and attire are attributed a unique flamboyance that successfully glamorizes the cherry blossom.

	4
1	
2	
3	

1 Cherry blossoms on a Makie lacquered inkstone case ⊙ CD 01_009
This rendition depicting of the cherry tree in full bloom imparts a sense of the gaiety of flower viewing.

2 Cherry blossom pattern on an embroidered long-sleeved kimono ⊙ CD 01_010
Easily rendered, the drooping cherry tree can be found in a variety of settings from attire to knick-knacks.

3 Drooping cherry tree blossoms rendered on an Urushie lacquered table ⊙ CD 01_011
The gently curving branch and the effluvient showy pink of the tips of the flowers and leaves depict one of the many facets of the cherry blossom.

4 Cherry blossoms rendered on a Makie lacquered inkstone case ⊙ CD 01_012
An accurately realistic depiction that offers an intellectual expression akin to the serene minds of people enjoying the view of yamazakura.

⊙ CD 01 013 – 016
Cherry Blossoms – 3

■ Falling cherry petals rendered on komon kimono
■ The only plant whose falling petals are considered a thing of beauty

Renditions of the eccentric and beautiful petals of fallen cherry blossoms

Although the fleeting lifespan of the cherry blossom is often the subject of poetry and song, patterns of falling cherry blossom petals are rarely found. Perhaps because even if the blooming cherry tree is accompanied by a small amount of falling petals, there is an underlying resistance among the Japanese people to the idea of things already "fallen". Be that as it may, the beauty of the patterns introduced here can hold its own against the splendor of any other pattern.

	4
1	
2	
3	

1 Komon kimono "kozakura" ⊙ CD 01_013
Though these patterns may be considered lovely, they do not impart a sense of the transience of the cherry blossom.

2 Komon kimono "scattered kozakura"
⊙ CD 01_014
An example of how the minor-key loudness of falling blossoms can be quelled by integrating strips of paper and hail.

3 Komon kimono " flowing cherry blossom filled water and young sweetfish" ⊙ CD 01_015
A beautifully structured design depicting how fallen cherry blossoms can be resurrected by the vibrancy of life.

4 Komon kimono " fallen cherry blossoms on tachiwaku" ⊙ CD 01_016
A signature komon pattern depicting the beautiful mold of cherry blossoms dispersed among dots. It was carved using a gimlet on a tachiwaku armorial insignia.

● CD 01 013 – 020
Wisteria

■ The personification of the Japanese sense of aesthetics
■ The expression of graceful floral hues and a self-effacing mood

The effect of a decorative pattern that preserves and stabilizes the balance between the "ears" of the wisteria's flowers

Though the Japanese people find the use of expressions such as "descend," "depart," and "scatter" to be taboo and therefore distasteful, with the hanging blossoms of the wisteria coupled with their elegant coloration one gets a sense more of modesty than pride, of blushing more than brazenness, and is conscious of the stability of the wisteria as a decorative pattern.

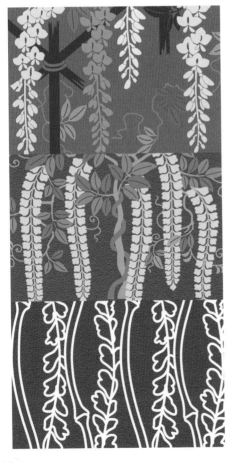

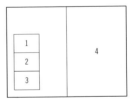

1 Wisteria trellis rendered in Chinese-style brocade
● CD 01_017
This rendition portrays wisteria with "ears" of diverse colors interwoven on a trellis to enhance the effect of the pattern.

2 Wisteria rendered on a gold brocade Noh costume
● CD 01_018
The symbolically trimmed ears of the wisteria flowers are visible even in their lilac lines, creating an easily evolving pattern.

3 Komon kimono "bamboo and wisteria pattern"
● CD 01_019
This tracing of wisteria flowers undulated by the wind on a tachiwaku armorial insignia provides a good example of the method.

4 Wisteria rendered on a mitsudae (litharge) painted box ● CD 01_020
A rare rendition, even among wisteria crests, depicting small wing petals peering out from behind large butterfly-shaped petals.

● CD 01 021 – 024

Peony – 1

- Celebrated even in China, the peony is a flower among flowers
- Considered an auspicious flower, the peony pattern is often included in renditions of deities and beasts (such as the Chinese lion-dog)

An opulent flower that forgives a consciously ornamental flamboyance

Referred to in China as "the king of one hundred flowers," any observer of the opulent form of the peony is left with a sense of "luxury and seduction." When rendered in design, the peony naturally assumes a lavish expression. Though excessive ornamentation tends to derogate from grace, one may also assert, of course, that in that expression there also exists an expression of intentional flamboyance.

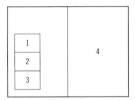

1	4
2	
3	

1 **An arabesque portrayal of the peony in an example of stencil and print dyed material** ● CD 01_021
This steadily rhythmic rendition of abundant petals offers a lesson in the kind of untutored expression observed only in the design and ornamental skill of Japan.

2 **An arabesque portrayal of peony on a Chinese-style embroidered "jimba" battle surcoat**
● CD 01_022
Imbued with elegance as a result of its repetitive motif, this peony pattern can also be used in regular design even though originally used as a form of battle dress.

3 **Peony rendered on old twill fabric** ● CD 01_023
The mold of this pattern has its origins in the simply designed flamboyance of the peony.

4 **Peony on a Chinese-style brocade Noh costume**
● CD 01_024
This rendition is ranked at the pinnacle of expression of peony design. There is a lot to learn from its timeless yet simple

● CD 01 025 – 028

Peony – 2

- Japanese pattern without the influences of Chinese design
- Design that imparts a sense of tranquility amidst flamboyance

A sophisticated Japanese sensitivity that has evolved from nobility to elegance

Though diverse examples of patterns greatly influenced by Chinese design can still be found in the midst of the peony motifs that exist today, Japan's unique sensitivity has caused the peony design pattern to evolve gradually from being regal to being sophisticatedly elegant. The peony pattern, which has changed with the progression of time, will eventually become a pattern free of both flamboyance and flowing elegance. Therein lies the peony's singular extravagance, the difficulty encountered in rendering the peony in design for common use.

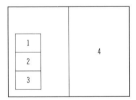

1 **Peony design rendered on Imari ware**
● CD 01_025
Though something of a paintinglike expression, this rendition has an expression that is unlike examples found in Chinese design.

2 **Peony rendered on a makie-lacquered inkstone case** ● CD 01_026
Though an example of realism, the designer can learn much from the economical expression of nature in this rendition.

3 **Komon kimono** ● CD 01_027
A rendition of peonies carved in small and large dots using a gimlet. One can sense the quietly observant eyes of our forefathers.

4 **Peony rendered on an urushie-lacquered tray**
● CD 01_028
One can feel the characteristic Japanese affinity to neatness and cleanliness in this rendition of the peony.

■ **Climbing rose rendered on a Yuzen print** ◉ CD 01_029 The rarity of the rose pattern suggests that the rose did not quite suit the Japanese sentiment. Though the "rose" of the Edo period was decidedly the peony, these leaves are undoubtedly that of the rose.

■ **A rendition of seedling ferns on a dyed light cotton summer kimono** ◉ CD 01_030 Though little more than seedling ferns rendered and scattered about in multiple layers, this design is prepossessing and devoid of any evidence of offensive expression.

Chapter 2
Plants/Summer

● CD 02 031 – 034

Summer Grasses

■ Excellent works even among the unusual summer grass patterns
■ Free expression unhindered by conventionality

Exuberant summer grasses simplified to communicate beauty

Some of the grass patterns of summer are rendered with a free-mindedness not encountered with the Japanese iris, vines (such as ivy, morning glory, bottle gourd, clematis), hollyhock, and so on used in ornamental design and family crests. The patterns introduced on this page in particular have an inspiring form that excites.

1	
2	4
3	

1 Lotus rendered on a plate in multicolored Kakiemon overglaze ● CD 02_031
This form of expression, remarkable for its delicate brushwork and use of colors, can be applied to a variety of designs.

2 Lilies rendered on a short-sleeved Yuzen print kimono ● CD 02_032
Renditions such as this require a sensitivity to such fine details as the pliancy of petals and leaves.

3 Hydrangea on a makie lacquered multi-tiered box ● CD 02_033
A bipolar expression of radiant hydrangea. This pattern offers insight into form.

4 Thistle rendered on a short-sleeved Yuzen print kimono ● CD 02_034
A fine example of the extent to which one can exquisitely render the form of a subject so difficult to render despite its beauty in the field.

● CD 02 035 – 038

Japanese Water Iris

■ A flower loved and appreciated by the aristocracy of dynasties
■ The sense of form in the streamlined shape of its flowers

The form of an elegant flower that continues to be loved by royalty

Siberian iris, water iris, and calamus share certain similarities. Their graceful and elegant appearances also display few differences. It becomes even more difficult to distinguish between the three flowers when rendered in patterns. No doubt these flowers were named to represent their uses with woven tools.

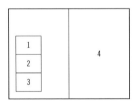

1 Water Iris rendered on an unlined kimono
● CD 02_035
The placement of its flowers will also influence one's ability to render clusters of water irises attractively.

2 Water iris on a flower pattern unlined kimono
● CD 02_036
Observe how each of the flowers in this bouquet of water iris is uniquely rendered.

3 Komon kimono "Water Iris" ● CD 02_037
Rendering the leaves of the water iris in layers to resemble a water crest provides the observer with hints as to form.

4 Water iris rendered on a short-sleeved yuzen print kimono ● CD 02_038
This undecorated rendition of graceful and delicate water iris is superb.

● CD 02 039 – 042

Ivy

■ A material often used in family crests in particular
■ A tangible image that is easy to render

Design that imparts more of a sense of wisdom and steadiness than of glamour

Suggestive of thriving progeny and prosperous business, the image of flourishing ivy is said to have been rendered as family crests and numerous other patterns. Their flowers aside, the charm of the vine lies mostly in the designlike shape of its "leaves". The fact that the vine can be made into attractive designs simply by adjusting positioning also makes it interesting.

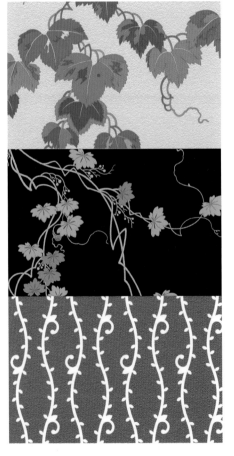

1	4
2	
3	

1 Ivy rendered on embroidery and foil-cloth
● CD 02_039
A timeless illustration of ivy on the verge of turning colors.

2 Ivy rendered on a makie lacquered multi-tiered box
● CD 02_040
The simplification of the veins of the leaves and the finely spun expression of the ivy teaches us how to handle the concept of body.

3 Komon kimono "vine tachiwaku" ● CD 02_041
There is an inevitability to the design of these vines fashioned after a tachiwaku armorial insignia.

4 Ivy rendered on a makie uchishiki alter cloth
● CD 02_042
Pertinent simplicity tells clearly of the intended use of this material.

⊙ CD 02 043 – 046

Clematis

- The patterns of these new flowers are also exotic
- These patterns are somewhat unsuited to the Japanese style of lyrical expression

The Clematis leaves room to enjoy the art of design

Since clematis is a relatively new flower imported from China early in the Edo Period, its unique nature quickly led to the creation of numerous patterns. Though some methods of pattern design do not impart the sense of "harmony", the combination of the unerring form of the flowers of the clematis with other elements has established the clematis as a pleasant pattern.

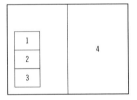

1 **Clematis rendered on a short-sleeved yuzen print crepe kimono** ⊙ CD 02_043
One's impression of this traditional yuzen insignia is dependent on how he perceives the few oddly rendered petals of the clematis.

2 **Arabesque clematis rendered on a Chinese-style brocade kimono** ⊙ CD 02_044
True to its other name, "arabesque," clematis has a slightly Chinese feel to it.

3 **Komon kimono "clematis"** ⊙ CD 02_045
This method of exploiting the characteristics of the vine to create a pattern provides many hints to its origin.

4 **Clematis rendered on a makie-lacquered tiered picnic box** ⊙ CD 02_046
Although this pattern feels a little ostentatious in some places, this rendering of beauty in design serves as an informative reference.

● CD 02 047 – 050
Morning Glory and Bottle Gourd

■ Summer flowers particularly loved by the common people
■ Their flowers, leaves, and vines are equally supple

Elegant patterns exuding an air of quietude and languidness

Morning glory and bottle gourd are inherently dissimilar plants. As the subject of design, these plants are beautiful vine flowers that both epitomize summer and impart the sense of a certain evanescence. Perhaps for these reasons, even patterns of these flowers that use diverse colors often have an atmosphere of beauty replete with tranquility and languor.

1		
2		4
3		

1 **Morning glory rendered on a Choken Noh costume**
● CD 02_047
The charm of this pattern resides in the harmony of the colors used in the rendition of the flowers and leaves to create a unified mood.

2 **Embroidered Noh costume** ● CD 02_048
One may observe the pure and tranquil expression as well as the curvature of the supple leaves.

3 **Komon kimono "calabash/bottle gourd"**
● CD 02_049
An evolving komon pattern where leaves and vines are unified and the bottle gourds are rendered in negative and positive fashion.

4 **Bottle gourd rendered on a makie-lacquered ink-stone case** ● CD 02_050
This rendition of harmony between flowers, leaves, and vines is superb.

● CD 02 051 – 054

Hollyhock

■ A traditional pattern made classical as a result of the origin of the insignia

Superior designability in the heart-shaped leaves and graceful flowers

Though the designs of hollyhock and arrowhead do not receive much attention today, they are found in abundance among traditional patterns. This is because in addition to being flowers that represent the social climate, there was a preference for beautiful designs containing both flowers and leaves like these. Often rendered together with water and as summer grass patterns, these flowers are indispensable for their pleasant image.

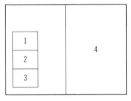

1	
2	4
3	

1 Hollyhock rendered on a short-sleeved Yuzen print kimono ● CD 02_051
Pay attention to this rendition that reminds one of the water's edge and give's one the sensation of the sunshine of summer.

2 Komon kimono "scattered hollyhock" ● CD 02_052
This deft rendition of the leaves of the hollyhock in positive and negative expression serves as a reference for methodology.

3 Komon kimono "hollyhock" ● CD 02_053
The simplification of the bi-lobed hollyhock and the expression of its flowers in dots can be made to evolve limitlessly through use and placement of color.

4 Hollyhock in flowing water rendered on a yuzen print ● CD 02_054
One is schooled in the design of pleasure by the lush expression of hollyhock in concert with flowing water.

● CD 02 055 – 058
Arrowhead

■ Patterns that remind us of the arrowheads adored by warriors
■ A summer material capable of expressing wisdom and bravery

Evolving form that should be utilized more in modern times

Also known as "Shogun-so (warlord grass)", the arrowhead shape of these flowers has a valiant air to it. Though idiosyncratic, their simple shapes gives breadth to form, and patterns of these flowers were often used as the family crests of samurai families.

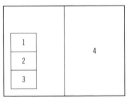

1 **Arrowhead rendered on a makie-lacquered chest**
● CD 02_055
Arrowheads at the ends of large swirls are beautiful in form when rendered collectively.

2 **Komon kimono "Arrowhead"** ● CD 02_056
A fine example of how inherently unique individual units retain their uniqueness, even when scattered without contrivance.

3 **Family crest "Arrowheads embracing offspring"**
"Arrowhead with five twists" ● CD 02_057
These patterns are remarkable for their forms that seem determined to surpass their existence as arrowheads.

4 **Arrowhead rendered on a makie-lacquered tray**
● CD 02_058
Appropriate to the aesthetic of utility, one's attention is drawn to this gently finished tray that avoids being overly angular.

■ **Komon kimono "Eggplant"** ● **CD 02_059** This background color goes by the Japanese name of "eggplant blue." Here, one is reminded of eggplants floating in a well in the heat of a summer day.

■ **Komon kimono "Fireworks"** ● **CD 02_060** Light, shape, and the summer activities where we enjoy sound are the themes of this design. These flowers of light are rendered in an intimate and nostalgic form that is also exuberant.

Chapter 3
Plants/Autumn

● CD 03 061 – 064

Autumn Grasses – 1

■ Autumn scenes that capture the hearts of the Japanese people
■ Autumn grasses that represent overabundant sentiment

Traditional patterns of autumn rendered as the counterparts of verse and song

As suggested by the saying, "Mono no aware wa aki zo masareru" (No other season epitomizes the miserable nature of things as excellently as autumn), written by the poet, Izumi Shikibu, autumn is celebrated in poetry and song more often than any of the other seasons. The same is true of the traditional patterns. These patterns, based on the themes of poetry and song, are more than mere decorative designs depicting the features of autumn. They are, rather, expressions of a sense of the season incorporated with a sentiment shared with poetry and song.

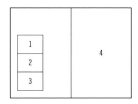

1 Dianthus rendered on embroidered foil-cloth
● CD 03_061
Though merely flowers and leaves that have been rendered as armorial insignias, this dainty and versatile rendition is also somewhat contemporary.

2 Dianthus and fence rendered on a short-sleeved kimono ● CD 03_062
There is much to learn from this rendition of the petals of the pink that gives the observer a sense of naturally adept expression.

3 Dragonfly and patrinia on a Choken Noh costume
● CD 03_063
As if to say that the song of insects and autumn fields go hand in hand, this is a good example of the storylike nature of autumn grasses rendered in design.

4 Moon and autumn grasses rendered on a kataginu robe ● CD 03_064
Observe how rendering the wildly blooming Chinese bellflower, patrina, and maiden grass in a single color keeps this piece from appearing chaotic.

● CD 03 065 – 068

Autumn Grasses – 2

- Flower fields of deep autumn in transition
- Memories alight on late autumn breezes

Descriptions of autumn filled with a pathos that strikes the heartstrings of the Japanese people

Autumn scenes expressed in traditional patterns are perceived as more than merely beautiful; they are endowed with a pathos that can be understood in the profound depths of our hearts. Perhaps this is because the echoes of autumn stimulate our heartstrings, lulling us with the tune of their afterglow. Those who embrace elegant aestheticism remain unchanged and are even now enticed by these images.

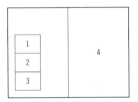

1 Kinpu flowering grasses ● CD 03_065
Though a generally delicate rendition, there is much to learn from this nonexcessively expressed design.

2 Silver grass rendered on an embroidered foil-cloth short-sleeved kimono ● CD 03_066
Although this is thought to be a Noh costume, one is surprised that such a method of rendering silver grass could be possible.

3 Begonia rendered in Chinese-style brocade ● CD 03_067
This example of brocade embroidery originating from China has not only been rendered with a sense of astringency, but has also entered the realm of elegant expression.

4 Autumn grasses rendered on a makie-lacquered multi-tiered box ● CD 03_068
Observe the superb balance in this rendition of bush clover, silver grass, patrinia, joe-pye weed, tartarian aster and so on swaying in the breeze.

● CD 03 069 – 072

Autumn Grasses – 3

■ From neat and tidy to florid expressions
■ Diverse renditions of freely conceived expressions of autumn grasses

The taste of autumn residing in brilliant expression

Not all of these patterns assume sentimentality simply because they are characterized as autumn grasses. The rendition of some patterns, depending on their subject matter, may require an expression of ornate beauty. Particularly in the case of "garments," a resonant harmony between purpose, weave, and expression is often observed in diverse renditions that, even so, do not lose that unique sense of autumn.

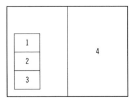

1 Bellflower rendered on an embroidered foil-cloth short-sleeved kimono ● CD 03_069
A variety of colored thread is used to successfully render chaotic impression in streamlined form.

2 Bellflower on a yuzen print short-sleeved kimono ● CD 03_070
In graceful and elegant expression one gets a sense of ethos and intimate passion.

3 Patrinia rendered on an embroidered foil-cloth short-sleeved kimono ● CD 03_071
Here, as with the bellflower rendered on an embroidered foil-cloth short-sleeved kimono, one has much to learn from this example of superior sense of design.

4 Bush clover and waterfall pattern rendered on a Yuzen print short-sleeved kimono ● CD 03_072
As if you can hear only the sound of water among the scene, try focusing your attention on this spatial rendition of an autumn field.

● CD 03 073 – 076
Chrysanthemum – 1

■ Another globally recognized national flower
■ The transition from natural to artificial beauty

A fundamental formative beauty that assumes a unique form of magic

The chrysanthemum integrated with autumn grasses has finally assumed the leading role as representative of autumn. When rendered as patterns in precise circles, the form of the chrysanthemum resembles the sun and has evolved flamboyantly with a formative beauty imbued with a special kind of magic in family crests, garments, and furnishings that epitomize Japan.

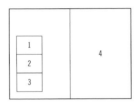

1 **A chrysanthemum bouquet rendered on a Choken Noh costume** ● CD 03_073
There is something interesting about this harmonization of chrysanthemum reminiscent of an armorial insignia combined with autumn grasses to form a single pattern.

2 **Chrysanthemum rendered on an embroidered foil-cloth short-sleeved kimono** ● CD 03_074
These vibrantly colored chrysanthemums have a unique symbolic beauty that cannot be attributed to autumn grasses.

3 **Arabesque chrysanthemum patterns rendered in Chinese-style brocade** ● CD 03_075
Both types of chrysanthemum have been rendered in circular shapes, implementing a contemporary technique of concentric circles to form an arabesque pattern.

4 **Chrysanthemum in water (kikusui) rendered on embroidered foil-cloth** ● CD 03_076
A masterpiece of artificial beauty epitomizing the legend of chrysanthemum immersed in water of perpetual youth and longevity.

⦿ CD 03 077 – 080
Chrysanthemum – 2

- Form perfectly rendered as the symbol of nobility
- Chrysanthemums are predominantly rendered as decorative flowers

The beauty of the chrysanthemum ranks particularly high even among the innumerable expressions of flowers

Though the Japanese people fundamentally adore natural beauty, the fact that they also have a love of the artificial beauty of the flower as something to be appreciated is testimony to the unique nature of the chrysanthemum. Their patterns are also rendered with a sense of the aesthetic of the chrysanthemum, giving birth to diverse chrysanthemum patterns of unique formative beauty.

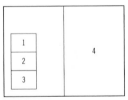

1 Medium-size chrysanthemum rendered on an unbelted women's outer garment (uchikake)
⦿ CD 03_077
Though clearly a chrysanthemum for appreciation unlike wild chrysanthemum, this rendition incorporates autumn grasses to impart a sense of nature.

2 Chrysanthemum rendered on short-sleeved kimono cloth ⦿ CD 03_078
In this rendition of somewhat realistic expression, the unbridled use of color as a means for enhancing design is overflowing with a sensitivity from which much can be learned.

3 Large-size chrysanthemum rendered on kimono
⦿ CD 03_079
This misshapen expression of chaotic large-size chrysanthemum is rendered in an expression which is rare among chrysanthemum patterns that are somewhat lacking in dynamism.

4 Chrysanthemum rendered on makie-lacquered furniture ⦿ CD 03_080
Observe the elaborate yet non-persisting sense of balance of these multi-layered large-size chrysanthemums.

⦿ CD 03 081 – 084
Chrysanthemum – 3

■ The chrysanthemum pattern observed through descriptive differences

Patterns that place their hopes in the intrinsic significance of the chrysanthemum

It is necessary to disrupt the symmetry of the evenly linked chrysanthemum petals in order to transform the so-called noble crests into patterns preferred by the common people. The realistic rendition of chrysanthemums blooming in fields is one example of how this is done. However, rather than focusing on dignity, these patterns exploit our faith in the traits of life prolongation, medicinal effect, good fortune, etc., with which the chrysanthemum is intrinsically endowed in their freely transforming, freely changing rendition.

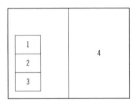

1 Chrysanthemum ring in stencil-dyed rendition
⦿ CD 03_081
The gentle expression of this stencil-dyed rendition has formed an endearing pattern of chrysanthemum.

2 Chrysanthemum and flowering grasses rendered on a lidded food container ⦿ CD 03_082
An autumn pattern in which chrysanthemums play the leading role.

3 Komon kimono (abundant chrysanthemum)
⦿ CD 03_083
Chrysanthemum flowers rendered in diverse expressions changing endlessly in kaleidoscopic patterns with the placement of colors.

4 Korin chrysanthemum rendered on a kataginu robe
⦿ CD 03_084
One is surprised by this peculiar mixture of abstractly rendered korin chrysanthemum and figuratively expressed leaves.

⬤ CD 03 085 – 088
Chrysanthemum – 4

- Chrysanthemum pattern variation observed in small patterns
- Diverse expression ranging from the sophisticated to the common

A highly diverse variety of patterns that appeals to the penchant of the common people

Evenly linking eight or more petal shapes has created numerous small pattern designs by ingeniously arranging the parts of the chrysanthemum flowers that are visible. Their evolving forms are endowed with limitless permutability through the combination of petal shapes, forms of linkage (circular, oval, and argyle shapes), sizes both large and small, colors, array, and other elements—catering to the preferences of the common people.

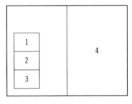

1 Komon kimono "chrysanthemum argyle"
⬤ CD 03_085
Argyle-shaped chrysanthemums are arrayed in unmatching layers in an expression suggestive of the fragrant embrace of the chrysanthemum.

2 Komon kimono "chrysanthemum and cherry blossom" ⬤ CD 03_086
A bright rendition, though reminiscent of the small patterns of spring when the chrysanthemum is viewed as similar to the Philadelphia daisy.

3 Komon kimono "chrysanthemum and bellflower"
⬤ CD 03_087
In this pattern it is easier to apply color to each flower and for the flowers to evolve than it would have been had the design been rendered in one color.

4 Komon kimono "chrysanthemum and butterfly"
⬤ CD 03_088
By virtue of being expressions of large-size chrysanthemums, even rendered on a large scale, these patterns form reasonably acceptable komon patterns.

● CD 03 089 – 092
Bush Clover

- A Japanese pattern that one may consider synonymous with autumn
- A flowering grass indispensable to the expression of autumn

The sight of delicate bush clover swaying in the wind is the very expression of autumn

Bush clover is classified essentially as shrubbery. From the fact that the kanji character for bush clover is written as the character for "autumn" crowned by the character representing "grass," one gets a sense of the profound nature of the sentiment of the ancients toward autumn.

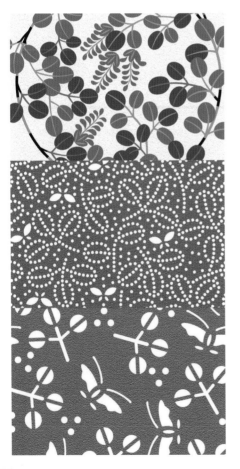

1	4
2	
3	

1 Bush clover rendered on a dyed cloth
● CD 03_089
Notice the balance in this rendition of supple, long branches gathered together in a delicate ring of flowers and leaves to form a single armorial insignia.

2 Komon kimono "bush clover and butterflies"
● CD 03_090
The way in which tool-carved butterflies accent the dots of bush clover leaves rendered using a gimlet is simply brilliant.

3 Komon kimono "bush clover and butterflies"
● CD 03_091
Though the title of this piece is the same as that of figure 2 above, this is a good example of how differing methods of expression can create images that are poles apart.

4 Bush clover rendered on an embroidered foil-cloth short-sleeved kimono ● CD 03_092
What a beautiful rendition of bush clover. This colorful example infallibly expresses another representation of autumn.

● CD 03 093 – 096

Turning Leaves

■ A feast of magnificent beauty to crown the ending of the season
■ Seen from a distance, these ornamental leaves are central to the pattern

Charm resides in their natural palmlike form

As epitomized by the maple tree, the brilliance of the turning leaves of autumn goes without saying. A single leaf taken in hand piques the appetite of the Japanese people with the all too designlike perfection of its natural form. And, of course, it cannot help but stir creative desire. In the world of decorative patterns, as well, numerous flamboyant works have been created that take advantage of the shape of the maple leaf.

1		4
2		
3		

1 Turning leaves of maple rendered on a makie-lacquered sake bottle ● CD 03_093
Tatsutagawa (a place described in Japanese verse) is a cornerstone of the momiji pattern. The contrast between the curving lines of the river and the acute angles of the leaves is brilliant.

2 Komon kimono "maple leaves and cherry blossoms" ● CD 03_094
A fine example that harnesses the tastes of the ancients in its simple expression of the cherry blossoms of spring and the maple leaves of autumn.

3 Komon kimono "Gingko" ● CD 03_095
The gingko is second only to the maple tree for the beauty of its autumn leaves. This piece has been inlcuded because of its unique pattern of contiguous curving lines carved using a gimlet

4 Turning leaves on an embroidered foil-cloth Noh costume ● CD 03_096
In this example of Ayanishiki there is a great deal to be learned from a vibrantly colored rendition that is quite different from realistic expression.

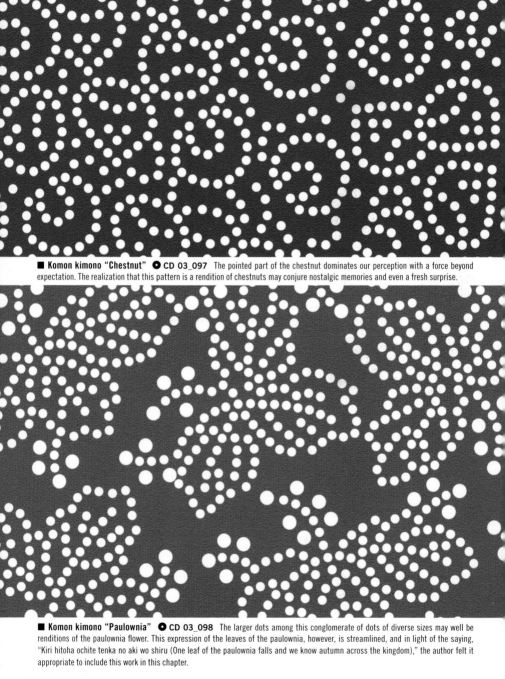

■ **Komon kimono "Chestnut"** ● **CD 03_097** The pointed part of the chestnut dominates our perception with a force beyond expectation. The realization that this pattern is a rendition of chestnuts may conjure nostalgic memories and even a fresh surprise.

■ **Komon kimono "Paulownia"** ● **CD 03_098** The larger dots among this conglomerate of dots of diverse sizes may well be renditions of the paulownia flower. This expression of the leaves of the paulownia, however, is streamlined, and in light of the saying, "Kiri hitoha ochite tenka no aki wo shiru (One leaf of the paulownia falls and we know autumn across the kingdom)," the author felt it appropriate to include this work in this chapter.

Chapter 4
Plants/Winter

CD 04 099 – 102

Camellia – 1

■ Pattern often religious in nature
■ These designs, including those of the meandering branches of the camellia tree, are of great importance

The beauty of camellia patterns that do not evoke the sense of recusal of the ancients

As if describing in written form the emotions of those who wait longingly for the coming of spring, when one observes the deep red of the camellia flower blooming just before the onset of spring, one is charmed by a beauty that seems to sweep away the flower's fateful tradition.

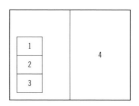

1 Camellia rendered on an urushi lacquerware bowl
 CD 04_099
One senses a kind of message in the powerful contrast of black on red lacquer in this rendition of camellia.

2 Camellia on a natsume tea caddy CD 04_100
Though the real item is rendered in makie-lacquer, this perfectly formed single pattern makes one want to apply additional colors.

3 Camellia rendered on a makie-lacquered inkstone case CD 04_101
Though the flowers of the camellia are delicate, there is an unmistakably vital energy expressed in the branches of the tree and the leaves on the whole.

4 Camellia rendered on a kamakura-style carved incense case CD 04_102
An expression of a flower worthy of being called voluptuous. This serves as a valuable lesson in the boldness of deformation.

● CD 04 103 – 106
Camellia – 2

■ Together with the pine tree, reverential of the life of the evergreen
■ Adoration of a flower blooming after enduring the severity of winter

The camellia, endowed with a profound ornamentality when rendered in design

More than a flower that blooms prior the onset of spring, the camellia has from time long past been considered a kind of spiritual tree that embodies the reverence of the Japanese people toward evergreen trees. As a result of the religious and magical influences derived from this perception, the camellia has been treated somewhat negatively as a flower. However, when observed purely from the perspective of design and form in traditional patterns, there are few flowers that are as richly ornate as the camellia.

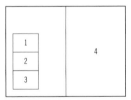

1 Camellia rendered on yuzen print fabric
● CD 04_103
Observe the sensation of unity, the form, and coloration of this seemingly unicursal rendition of camellia.

2 Camellia rendered on an embroidered foil-cloth sash ● CD 04_104
Much can be learned from the strong literary sense perceived in a free and unconstrained expression shared by the Korin plum tree and the pine tree.

3 Camellia rendered on a makie-lacquered multi-tiered box ● CD 04_105
One cannot ignore the presence of the camellia as the main character in this altered rendition of a bouquet of camellia in a flower basket.

4 Camellia on the garments of a lady-in-waiting
● CD 04_106
The original item is an excellent example of descriptive power with forceful brush strokes. This method gives one a sense of the superb life force of the camellia.

⬤ CD 04 107 – 110
Daffodils

- A delicate flower swaying in cold winds
- A posture that imparts purity and intellect

A flower not easily rendered in design

Pure white petals and a full stamen. Together with the deep-green of its free and easy leaves, these attributes alone are virtually enough to be considered a complete and beautiful design. As such, failing to render even one of these essential points will cause the daffodil to resemble something quite different from the flower that it is. Herein lies the difficulty encountered in the development of these flowers as design. Even among the traditional patterns, while all pieces are high-quality works, there are many patterns that are similar in form.

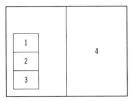

1 Daffodil rendered on a makie-lacquered tray
⬤ CD 04_107
Observe the rendition and good balance of the flowing curves of the long and languid leaves.

2 Daffodil rendered on a short-sleeved yuzen print kimono ⬤ CD 04_108
The delicacy of these daffodils is more a slightly mundane expression that hints at "innocence."

3 Komon kimono "Argyle with daffodil pattern trellis" ⬤ CD 04_109
A rendition of small patterns that retains the immaculate beauty of the daffodil.

4 Daffodils rendered on a plate decorated in nabeshima overglaze enamels ⬤ CD 04_110
The pristine and unvarnished expression and the leaves arranged to match the curvature of the plate in this superb rendition offers a lot to be learned.

● CD 04 111 – 114
Plum-1

■ Modest flowers that bloom in intense cold
■ A diverse variety of expression patterns

Used for a number of purposes, the plum is a recognized representative patterns

At the time that these traditional patterns were established, when one spoke of "flowers," it was the "flowers of the plum tree" to which they referred. Originating from China, plum flowers were adored by nobility and commonfolk alike. Testimony to this is the diverse array of plum patterns found in different colors and shapes, from luxury products to everyday knick knacks, that have been created.

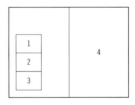

1 Plum rendered on a yuzen print short-sleeved kimono ● CD 04_111
This somewhat planar rendition of deforme plum flowers and branches expresses gentleness.

2 Plum on a mother-of-pearl box ● CD 04_112
One perceives a highly advanced artistic sense in the harmony achieved between the shapes of the flowers, the buds, and the branches.

3 Seaside plum rendered on a short-sleeved kimono ● CD 04_113
This radically symbolic rendition of a wave crest is stimulated by a rich conceptualization from which the Korin plum is developed.

4 Plum tree rendered on a kanoko-dyed long-sleeved kimono ● CD 04_114
This rendition of a patterned plum tree with branches in fluid formation and the division of color is a superlative expression of space.

⦿ CD 04 115 – 118

Plum – 2

■ The perpetual permutation of designs made possible by their simple form
■ Patterns that render the diversity of expression in easy-to-understand fashion

Rounded links that are simple, yet able to provoke creativity

Five circles can be linked together to create the form of the plum flower. The fact that no two works among the innumerable plum patterns are the same is testimony not only to the topical visual diversity seen in the rendition of colors, shape, and descriptive method, but also to the diverse nature of the intended images of their creators.

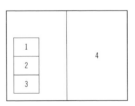

1 Plum rendered on a transom ⦿ CD 04_115
A rendition of plum blossoms that have not particular charm. Its uniqueness rests in the integration of old wood within the frame of the transom.

2 Rounded plum rendered on dyed fabric
⦿ CD 04_116
Though the petals are not especially remarkable, this rendition surmounts stereotype by adding diversity to the stamens.

3 Komon kimono "plum and bush warbler"
⦿ CD 04_117
Using branches to link the plum blossoms and distribute bush warblers throughout, transform this rendition into a unique pattern.

4 Plum rendered on a makie-lacquered letterbox
⦿ CD 04_118
The straightforward form of the plum, rendered in monotone, appears surreal and unique.

● CD 04 119 – 122
Plum – 3

- A collection of patterns where each plum blossom is uniquely rendered
- The elements of elegance, color, and fragrance

Plum patterns that give one a sense of the limitless possibilities of expression

Since the era of *Myriad Leaves*, when Japan's sentiment toward the elegance, hue, and fragrance of the plum blossom which had established themselves in our hearts came to be rendered as form, a greater number of plum patterns were created. And when the plum crest became popular as family insignias, the creation of unique plum blossoms expanded the world of the plum pattern even more.

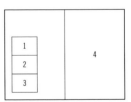

1 Komon kimono "plum" ● CD 04_119
Rendering the representative plum insignia as a small pattern design has given birth to a refined gimlet-carved dot expression.

2 Komon kimono "plum pot" ● CD 04_120
This teaches of the appeal of scattering single units of armorial insignia to form a different insignia.

3 Komon kimono "fallen pine, bamboo and plum"
● CD 04_121
A unique rendition of plum blossoms formed by using a gimlet to carve small plum flowers inside the petals of a plum insignia.

4 Komon kimono "scattered small flower pattern"
● CD 04_122
Though this design is a rendition of komon, it is also an expression of form that bears appreciation even if the flowers are rendered as large patterns.

⊙ CD 04 123 – 126
Pine

- The concept of "pine" in original Japanese interpretation
- Views of pine that enrich our lives

A collection of patterns that represent the sophisticated spiritual culture of the ancients

The fondness that the Japanese people have toward the pine, which remains constant throughout the four seasons, need not be expressed in words after all this time. It would be no exaggeration to say that the scenes of pine depicted in traditional patterns represent the profound spiritual culture of the ancients. This is graphically telling in well-polished and overwhelming artistry.

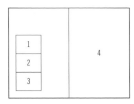

1 **Pine rendered on an unlined kimono**
⊙ CD 04_123
This rendition of pine, which is often depicted in stately fashion, is a colorful and lightly designed picture.

2 **Pine rendered on an oribe glaze mukozuke dish**
⊙ CD 04_124
A fine example of how affinity and profound spirituality is expressed through motif.

3 **Komon kimono "pine"** ⊙ CD 04_125
A good example of the use of gimlet carving to render a very stylized pine insignia, scattering the patterns to create a different atmosphere for the pine.

4 **Pine rendered on a makie-lacquered small box**
⊙ CD 04_126
This portrayal of pine leaves is a preview of the style of pine to be later rendered as armorial insignia.

● CD 04 127 – 130
Bamboo

■ The bamboo is reminiscent of refreshing dynamism
■ The ever-changing demeanor of bamboo rendered erect and pliable

Patterns depicting the effort put into expressing the tall figure of bamboo

The attributes of bamboo have been widely used as tools in daily life since ancient times. Since it is difficult to render the tall figure of bamboo in the composition of design, it is often found as decorative design on garments of longer lengths. Otherwise, it is often rendered as bamboo grass.

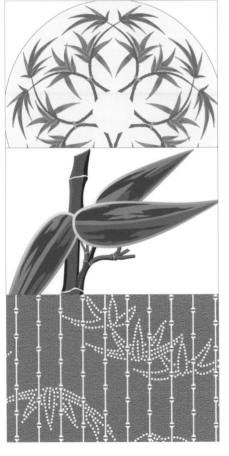

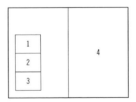

1 Bamboo rendered on a plate decorated in nabeshima overglaze enamels ● CD 04_127
Though this does not depict the rigidity of the bamboo, this piece serves as a reference to the many possibilities for the evolution of form.

2 Bamboo rendered on a cloissone nail head cover ● CD 04_128
This sensitive depiction focused on the leaves of the bamboo teaches us a method of expression that exploits the beauty of purposeful utility.

3 Komon kimono "bamboo stripes" ● CD 04_129
The appeal of this contrast resides in the amazing sensitivity of a creator who has rendered a work made possible only for its use of bamboo.

4 Bamboo rendered on silk wrapping cloth ● CD 04_130
Though the contrast is slightly strong, this rendition depicts the many expressions of the bamboo.

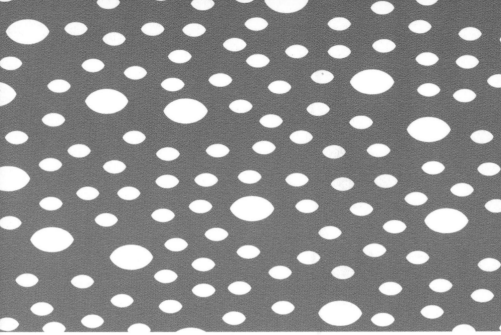

■ **Komon kimono "cylindrical semi-circular hail"** ● CD 04_131 Though namako refers to a cylindrical semi-circular shape, this rendition could also be said to express large and small eye-shaped hail. This pattern may appear as a painful expression when observed vertically and a rough pattern when viewed diagonally.

■ **Komon kimono "dew-drenched grass and bundles of straw"** ● CD 04_132 Only in an extremely relaxed state could one have the emotional comfort to render such subject matter in design.

Chapter 5
Creatures

⏺ CD 05 133 – 136
Birds

■ Adoration for the figure of the bird flying freely through the air
■ Birds signifying auspicious signs, military spirit, and more

Often renditions of realistic expression, these designs can be somewhat difficult to use in contemporary design

The crane, which is considered an auspicious bird, is often found among bird patterns. In design, eagles, hawks, and mandarin ducks are rendered as spectacular, while plovers, sparrows, and swallows, are depicted as lovely birds. Since bird patterns are generally realistic expressions and difficult to use in contemporary design, this chapter will introduce the more expansive examples.

1	4
2	
3	

1 Komon kimono "flying cranes" ⏺ CD 05_133
Observe the light touch rarely found in bird patterns and the more beautiful simplicity.

2 Chumon "willow and sparrow" ⏺ CD 05_134
This design of sparrows gathering among branches of willow is superb. None of the sparrows suffer by comparison with any of the others.

3 Komon kimono "plovers" ⏺ CD 05_135
These lovely plovers are rendered naturally in a design made more effective by their uncontrived placement.

4 Waves and plovers rendered on a kyogen costume
⏺ CD 05_136
Waves are exquisitely balanced, and together with the plovers, overflow with dynamic beauty in this contemporary pattern.

● **CD 05** 137 – 140

Insects

■ A soft material aiming at a new kind of pattern expression
■ The changing form of the highly popular and overwhelmingly abundant butterfly

The elegantly dancing form of beautifully colored butterflies and the endlessly evolving nature of design

In the world of patterns, one is always inclined to select materials that are pleasing to the eye. In order to impart the appearance of autumn as elegantly as possible, some patterns are decorated with autumn grasses and singing insects. Ultimately, from the perspective of their beauty in flight and evolvability of design, no other subject matter surpasses the butterfly.

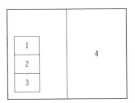

1 Komon kimono "winning insect" ● CD 05_137
These simplified dragonflies are winsome, rendered in a random array as if no other method could have been conceivable.

2 Komon kimono "butterfly" ● CD 05_138
Though the concept here is the same as the "winning insect" described in figure 1 above, one gets the impression that this rendition could benefit from slightly fewer butterflies.

3 Komon kimono "butterfly stripes" ● CD 05_139
Looking at this pattern, one gets a hint of the possibilities of endlessly extending stripe patterns.

4 Komon kimono "silver grass and butterflies"
● CD 05_140
Unique for uniform round dots formed using a gimlet, the strong points of these alien-like materials lie less in their assertiveness than in the impression they give when observed from a distance.

● CD 05 141 – 144
Fish and Animals

■ A feeling for materials selected for specific uses
■ The story of using materials mindful of tools

Untold significance inherent in traditional patterns that continue to exist today

Shrimp represented long life, the fox was the emissary of the gods, the bat was thought to be the herald of fortune, and the carp was the symbol of success… The ancients selected a diverse array of creatures from the universe in which to entrust their happiness. For this reason, even in contemporary times one feels somewhat uncomfortable with designs that confound the significance and tools of tradition.

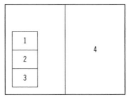

1 Komon kimono "shrimp" ● CD 05_141
From the layout it seems as if the shrimp are jumping. Effectively combining this rendition with waves would perhaps add additional appeal.

2 Komon kimono "fox" ● CD 05_142
Could the foxes be running about in the snow? This gaiety inspiring picture does away with the slightly negative image of the fox.

3 Komon kimono "bat" ● CD 05_143
Like the "Fox" in figure 2 above, this rendition also lacks negativity, and its uniqueness as a pattern even offers insight into the tricks of the designer's trade.

4 Chumon "circular carp and peony"
● CD 05_144
One mistaken brushstroke alone could transform this design into a tasteless work. It would benefit from a slightly more ingenious integration of materials.

■ **Komon kimono "crane and turtle among a variety of treasures"** ◉ CD O5_145 Perhaps the cranes and turtles, bags of treasure, lucky mallets, pine, bamboo, balls, and cloves will be measured against bundo weights (units shaped like eyes). When one begins to question why there are no hooks and umbrellas, this work becomes a lively pattern that could tell tales.

■ **Komon kimono "water and rain dragon pattern"** ◉ CD O5_146 Though dragons are imaginary animals of fortune thought to reside in lakes, swamps, and the ocean, rising into the sky on occasion to evoke rain from the clouds, they have appeared often in design. Rain and the dragon exist together like a pair.

Chapter 6
Waves/Flowing Water

● CD 06 147 – 150
Waves and Flowing Water – 1

- Elegance possible only in this land of oceans and fields overgrown with reeds
- The temporal beauty of the momentary transformation of water

The strength of traditional design is indispensable to the expression of water

Scenes of the oceans and rivers are so pervasive in the Japanese mind that they are taken for granted. Consequently, when the need to render water arises, establishing its extremely free and difficult to grasp existence in design can be rather difficult without taking an extremely careful approach. At such times one feels the need to refer to the spirituality and form of the water patterns handed down to us by our ancestors.

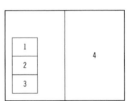

1	4
2	
3	

1 Waves rendered on a short-sleeved embroidered yuzen print kimono ● CD 06_147
Though seemingly insignificant, the ripples and foam wave crests depict shallows with a tranquil atmosphere.

2 Flowing water rendered on a short-sleeved yuzen print kimono ● CD 06_148
When shown such an image of flowing water, one loses all hesitancy toward the shape of the subject on which the pattern is to be rendered and feels empowered to create.

3 Waves rendered on a short-sleeved yuzen print kimono ● CD 06_149
Though the same can be said of figure 2, through this piece one gets the sense of space in a profound spirituality that belies the simplicity of its own rendition.

4 Waves rendered on a patterned short-sleeved kimono ● CD 06_150
A collection of unhesitatingly elegant lines superimposed with rhythmical wave crests. A masterpiece from which one does not sense the hard work that went into its creation.

● **CD 06** 151 – 154

Waves and Flowing Water – 2

■ The truth of waves that bring to mind a powerful reason
■ The abstraction of essence rendered through methodology of expression

A high-quality finished form realized solely through the design of the waves

As is the case with the four examples introduced here, waves rendered in traditional patterns are not always depicted alone, but are rather accompanied by floating flowers, the turning leaves of autumn, boats, rabbits, and other elements. If one were to compare a wave pattern stripped of its accompanying elements to its original form, he or she would be surprised at the beauty made whole by the design of the waves alone.

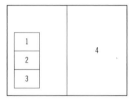

1 **Waves rendered on a makie-lacquered garment box cover** ● CD 06_151
A lidded container for storing and transporting folded kimonos. Rendering the container itself to resemble water imparts a refreshing mood.

2 **Waves rendered on a makie-lacquered tiered picnic box** ● CD 06_152
The actual piece depicts a plover resting on a wave crest. This is such an excellent example of skill in forming the wave pattern that the bird feels superfluous.

3 **Waves rendered on a makie-lacquered sake bottle** ● CD 06_153
One wonders if the owner used to pour sake into this sake bottle to carry with him on excursions for flower viewing or viewing the turning of autumn leaves. The original work depicts turning leaves rendered with the flowing water of Tatsutagawa. Observing the waves without their accompanying elements gives one the impression that he or she is viewing the streamlined form of an abstract painting.

4 **Flowing water rendered on a makie-lacquered flower viewing lunchbox** ● CD 06_154
In this rendition, the lines are even more refined than those in figure 3 above. A line of wave crests come together to create a break in this sharply cutting depiction of flowing water.

● CD 06 155 – 158

Waves and Flowing Water – 3

■ Renditions of waves that require powerful techniques to create a design transformed by desire
■ Waves give us clues as to how to escape formalized beauty

Traditional patterns that school us in love for and observation of flowing water

"Yuku kawa no nagare-wa taezushite, shikamo moto no mizu ni arazu." (The flow of the river is ceaseless and its water is never the same.) As suggested by this saying by poet Kamo no Chomei, as quickly as flow manifests itself in form and sentiment in the back of our minds, just as quickly do those manifestations disappear.

1	4
2	
3	

1 Flowing water rendered on a makie-lacquered inkstone case ● CD 06_155
An almost completely abstract rendition of flowing water, this piece teaches us how to grasp the points that make one want to say "I am certain I have seen this type of water insignia before."

2 Waves rendered on colored paper ● CD 06_156
This is the most typically Japanese and well-known example of the wave. How many designers have created renditions evolved from these waves?

3 Komon kimono "flowing water" ● CD 06_157
Looking at this pattern, we are taught that "there is no particular need to exert oneself anew."

4 Flowing water rendered on the cover of a book of Noh songs ● CD 06_158
Compliments to the philosophical completeness of this attempt to make the freely flowing nature of the water our own, as suggested by the name of this pattern, "tomoemizu" (or swirling waters).

● CD 06 159 – 162

Waves and Flowing Water – 4

- Brilliant patterns that transform turbulent waves into a world of tranquility
- Methods of describing temporal moments in the movement of water

The form of the curvatures of the waves are the key factors in expressing the athleticism of the wave crests

Though designs of wave crests rendered as pattern are by no means rare, any new wave creation must express the shape of wave crests influenced by the moving curves of the water that precedes them. Otherwise, no matter how much the rendition may resemble a wave in form, it will not impart the sense of the dynamism of the wave. The waves of traditional patterns do an excellent job of this.

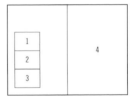

1 Waves on a makie-lacquered inkstone case
● CD 06_159
In this rendition, a visually rhythmic pattern is repeated to create an excellent expression of the dynamic beauty of the wave.

2 Waves rendered on a makie-lacquered wooden tray ● CD 06_160
This rendition focuses on the interesting nature of fleeting wave crests. We can learn from this example in which waves are rendered in both close and distant expressions.

3 Waves on a lacquered mother-of-pearl pot
● CD 06_161
While at first glance this depiction shows the inverted roll of the waves with a violent expression, the fact that it does not feel unnatural is fascinating.

4 Waves rendered on a makie-lacquered chest
● CD 06_162
A masterpiece of dynamic wave crests seemingly induced by the curves of the surface layers of the waves in an expression that beckons the next wave to follow.

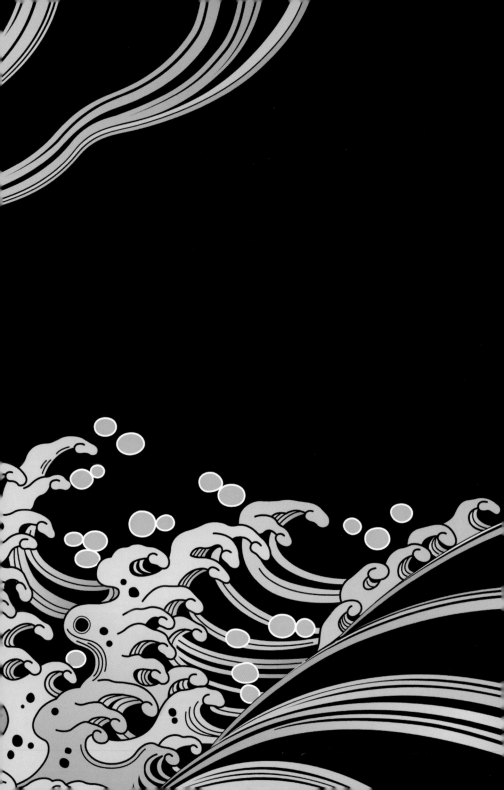

● CD 06 163 – 166

Waves and Flowing Water – 5

■ Japan's most celebrated masterpiece of the wave pattern, seigaiha
■ The wave theme of diversely changing and evolving form

Concepts founded on the basics produce limitless, original wave patterns

Seigaiha patterns are commonplace today. No other pattern has such chaotic beauty—or so beautifully crashes—no matter how the pattern has evolved as long as the basic rules are observed. Surely no other geometrical pattern themes would benefit from these characteristics. To form your own concepts you may want to revisit the wave insignias rendered with the three lines that are most basic to the seigaiha.

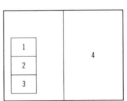

1 **Evolving seigaiha rendered in Chinese-style brocade** ● CD 06_163
Though evolutions of seigaiha this sophisticated pattern is classified in a special category of design. This piece is beneficial to the study of conceptual freedom.

2 **Seigaiha on a Choken Noh costume** ● CD 06_164
A tasteful and refined rendition of seigaiha. There is an indescribable elegance to the waveforms that consists of two curved lines.

3 **Komon kimono "seigaiha and plover"**
● CD 06_165
Plovers are placed inside the gaps formed by dividing units of seigaiha. Such aspects were probably the starting point of the conceptualization of this work.

4 **Waves rendered on an embroidered foil-cloth costume** ● CD 06_166
The original work is a dazzling, luxurious garment pattern depicting the phoenix and mandarin ducks atop the waves. Although an item of this level can no longer be referred to as seigaiha, without a doubt, this example adheres to the chaotic style of seigaiha to form elegant waves that are full of life.

⦿ **CD 06** 167 – 170

Waves and Flowing Water – 6

■ Highly unique renditions of waves and flowing water developed by creators of arts and crafts
■ Excellent works of traditional design that cultivate creative skill

A boldness capable of capturing a single moment of dynamism, a self-possessed perspective capable of reproducing flow

Though the waves rendered by these artists certainly need no commentary at this point, these examples have achieved a mastery that is unique. Furthermore, they charm their innumerable admirers. The almost too famous waves of artists such as Katsushika Hokusai are not introduced here. This is because we could never achieve greater heights no matter how much we refer to these masters' works. One is charmed, however, simply by observing the examples presented here.

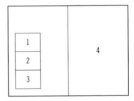

1 **Waves rendered on a ninsei tea cup**
⦿ CD 06_167
Observe this rendition that reminds you of the water's edge and give's one the sensation of the sunshine of summer.

2 **Flowing water rendered on korin kohaku umezu**
⦿ CD 06_168
This deft rendition of the leaves of the hollyhock in positive and negative expression serves as a reference for methodology.

3 **Wave rendered in a Hokusai cartoon**
⦿ CD 06_169
Katsushika Hokusi and Utagawa Hiroshige are both renown ukio-e masters. This wave is a section of waves rendered in a cartoon.

4 **Wave crests rendered by Ito Jakuchu**
⦿ CD 06_170
Ito Jakuchu, a mid-Edo Period cartoonist. Waves rendered in one section of "Phoenix in the Rising Sun" (Asahi hoo-zu).

● CD 06 171 – 174

Waves and Flowing Water – 7

■ Renditions that do away with the grave dignity encountered in garments
■ Dynamic yet not overly light expression

Wave and flowing water patterns arouse our awareness of beautifully curving lines

The waves encountered in garments are often rendered as a part of the scenery. All the more reason that we tend to overlook the interesting aspects of waveform when we observe the other themes presented. Extracting only the waves as we have done here allows us to reaffirm the beauty inherent in their curvature.

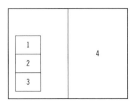

1 Waves rendered on a short-sleeved crepe kimono
● CD 06_171
Rendered in carefree and elegant curves, these waves avoid being violent and have a gentleness suitable for use with garments.

2 Waves rendered on a kaga yuzen print short-sleeved kimono ● CD 06_172
The dynamics of the waves create a beautiful harmony even as this work retains the trademark yuzen obfuscation.

3 Waves rendered on suo men's kimono
● CD 06_173
A garment worn by the warriors of Kyogen. The bold expression of seigaiha-style realistic form of waves viewed from close proximity serves as a reference to form.

4 Waves rendered on a stencil-dyed unlined kimono
● CD 06_174
The slightly hushed waves rendered using the stencil-dye method are interesting and do a good job of expressing the characteristics of the dyeing technique.

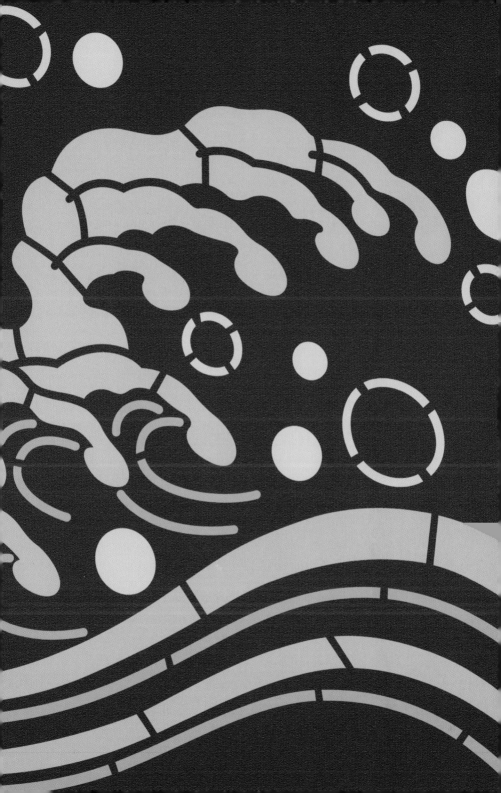

■ **Waves rendered on an unbelted women's garment** ● CD 06_175   From the wave crests, whose curvature could be referred to as the Bohemian expression of ocean waves, one is schooled in the state of the free and intellectual mind.

■ **Waves rendered using the stencil-dye technique** ● **CD 06_176** A carefree and elegant wave pattern. The skilled lines borne of an unerring carver's sword.

■ **Wave crest rendered on a twill Noh costume** ● **CD 06_177** The excellent observant eye of the ancients is rendered here in such unique form that one look will render it absolutely unforgettable.

Chapter 7
Arabesque

● CD 07 178 – 181
Arabesque – 1

■ The arabesque pattern is stately and majestic

A collection of honeysuckle-like arabesque patterns frequently observed in Buddhist designs

Japan's classical arabesque designs are often found in images of the Buddha, the canon, architecture, and other Buddhist products. While generally disciples of the honeysuckle arabesque pattern, there are as many variations of rhythm, terminal curvature, thickness, mood, twist and linkage as there are things Japanese. There is perhaps no other pattern that demonstrates more ornamental and evolutionary traits.

1	
2	4
3	

1 Mandorla on an eleven-headed Kannon statue
● CD 07_178
Though the form of the mandorla itself is unique, its multi-layered arabesque expression is also majestic.

2 The center portion of a copper mirror "honey-suckle arabesque" ● CD 07_179
Simplifying and organizing the lines creates a complete units of patterns that can be used even in contemporary design.

3 Embroidered Noh costume "honeysuckle arabesque" ● CD 07_180
Shedding its Chinese influences, this beautiful arabesque pattern is rendered with a sensitivity unique to Japan.

4 The mandorla portion of a non-flying Kannon statue "honeysuckle arabesque" ● CD 07_181
A three-dimensionally carved example. As a manual for the rendition of form, the continuity of this arabesque pattern is natural and streamlined.

● CD 07 182 – 185

Arabesque – 2

■ Patterns passed down from China that have been remarkably transformed to suit the sensibilities of the Japanese people
■ Unique names given to patterns to match the classification of their motifs

The life force of vines entrusted with our aspirations rendered in auspicious patterns

In addition to vines, arabesque patterns also use flowers, leaves, and fruit as the subject of motifs, thus incorporating a wide variety of plants in their designs. Patterns are classified as peony arabesque or chrysanthemum arabesque, and so on, depending on the type of motif. Considered symbols of longevity, the proliferous vines are used widely as an auspicious design.

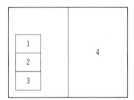

1 **Indigo blue cotton fabric dyed using a pattern overlay "cherry blossom arabesque"** ● CD 07_182
This is an excellent example of Japanese-style arabesque rendered in a pattern of sophisticated and refined beauty.

2 **Indigo blue cotton fabric dyed using a pattern overlay "chrysanthemum arabesque"** ● CD 07_183
The stems and leaves of the chrysanthemum formed in arabesque patterns are a good example of how normally unthinkable subject matter can be rendered in design.

3 **Makie-lacquered tea case "Chinese flower pattern arabesque"** ● CD 07_184
While one could point out the influences of Chinese decoration techniques on the form of this Chinese flower pattern, there is no overlooking the overall Japanese quality of its beauty.

4 **Indigo blue cotton fabric dyed using a pattern overlay "peony arabesque"** ● CD 07_185
This quiet yet amiable design, where color is applied to the vines, takes full advantage of the characteristics of pattern overlay dyeing methods. It is brilliant.

CD 07 186 – 189

Arabesque – 3

■ Arabesque patterns that have evolved into uniquely Japanese patterns
■ Techniques of expression unique to Japanese dyeing methods

The diverse ornamental qualities of the arabesque pattern stimulates the sensitivity of designers

The classical arabesque patterns of contemporary Japan were handed down from China, and – if one were to venture even further into the depths of history – most likely had originated with the nations along the Silk Road. Their diverse ornamental qualities inspire the sensitivities of Japanese designers. Over time, these patterns have achieved a completeness and transformation that are completely unique to Japan.

1 Indigo blue dyed pattern "wild chrysanthemum arabesque" ● CD 07_186
Though simple, this is the kind of frank work of profound aesthetics loved by the Japanese people.

2 Indigo blue dyed pattern "peony arabesque" ● CD 07_187
The simplification of the veins of the leaves and the finely spun expression of the ivy teaches us how to handle the concept of body.

3 Indigo blue dyed pattern "lion's mane arabesque" ● CD 07_188
No matter what material is used, one is empowered by this method that uses the qualities of the material to create independent patterns.

4 Indigo blue dyed pattern "chrysanthemum arabesque" ● CD 07_189
This example of an amply comfortable configuration and frank yet elegant descriptive method should be used widely as a reference.

⏺ CD 07 190 – 193

Arabesque – 4

■ Endearing decorative patterns popular even among the general public
■ A uniquely Japanese sense of nature that gives birth to variation

Advancements in dyeing techniques have given "arabesque" patterns mass appeal

The numerous patterns created since arabesque patterns came to be known simply as "arabesque," consequently assuming a more "common" aspect, are not completely unrelated to advancements in dyeing techniques. Though the art of dyeing is part of the larger category of "graphic arts," the advancements made in dyeing techniques have increased the pace of the spread of popular items and increased variation among designers.

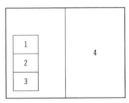

1 Indigo blue dyed pattern "lion's mane arabesque" ⏺ CD 07_190
An example of lion's mane arabesque expressed with great precision. Commonplace and appealing to the masses, but also dignified.

2 Stencil-dyed pattern "dots and arabesque" ⏺ CD 07_191
It is not clear how to classify this example of arabesque design. However, the dots rendered in contrast to the arabesque pattern are living examples of evolving form.

3 Stencil-dyed pattern "octopus arabesque" ⏺ CD 07_192
The fact that octopus legs rendered in arabesque form have been used in ceramic works produced in the Kutani-yaki and Imari-yaki schools of pottery is testimony to the depth of the freedom enjoyed by the Japanese people.

4 Indigo blue fabric dyed using a pattern overlay "chrysanthemum arabesque" ⏺ CD 07_193
This shows chrysanthemum precisely rendered by alternating the base colors. A bold yet not overpowering example of elegant arabesque patterns.

◉ **CD 07** 194 – 197

Arabesque – 5

■ The transition from normal arabesque to normal flower patterns
■ The sense of the possibilities of variation

Innovative designs that exploit the rhythm of arabesque patterns

A new form of design that takes advantage of the rhythm of the arabesque pattern to form arabesque motifs that do not feel "arabesque" has also been developed. Unlike the rhythm of the undulating curvature of the vines introduced thus far, these are pretty and refined arabesque patterns similar to the usual flower patterns.

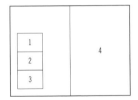

1 Dyed pattern "Chinese flower arabesque"
◉ CD 07_194
The flowers used here give this rendition a slightly religious feel. However, the curvature of the branches and leaves and repeating units of design makes this an innovative arabesque pattern.

2 Kyo Karakami fusuma paper "(boke) arabesque"
◉ CD 07_195
Light and pretty form from which diverse variations could easily evolve.

3 Kyo Karakami fusuma paper "primrose arabesque" ◉ CD 07_196
Viewed in this way, one gets the impression that any flower could be rendered in arabesque form, giving breadth to the conceptualization of the flower in design.

4 A lacquered hot water pot "Chinese flower arabesque" ◉ CD 07_197
An attractive contemporary design. One may learn much from the streamlined rendition of the proliferating leaves and branches of the vine.

■ **Arabesque bellflower rendered on a cotton garment** ● CD 07_198   Here, these two forms of arabesque patterns have created a two distinct renditions of arabesque vines and arabesque leaves and flowers. There are surprisingly many arabesque patterns where the main object (flowers) seems to have been added after the arabesque background was created.

■ **Stencil-dyed arabesque hollyhock** ● CD 07_199   This type of karakusa pattern is intended to bury the main subject in the curvature of arabesque patterns. It has a very different significance for the woven pattern from that of arabesque patterns in which the vines, flowers, and leaves are integrated as one. Therefore, the arabesque vines themselves do not express any traits that would make them a focal point in this rendition.

Chapter 8
Geometry

⦿ CD 08 200 – 203

Stripes – 1

■ Straight and curved lines that form design
■ A unique Japanese world developed from an integration of methods of embroidery and dyeing

Simple and straightforward patterns that reached the height of popularity as the brilliance of the Edo Period

Of all the geometric stripe patterns, Japanese people feel the greatest affinity for the Japanese stripe design rendered on the kimono. Without particular focus on the flower, bird, wind, or moon motifs, these patterns only use lines to establish themselves against the backdrop of the culture of the townspeople of Edo. Straight lines are boldly distributed to form simple yet powerful configurations that have no equal.

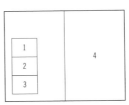

1 Shikan stripe pattern ⦿ CD 08_200
A stripe pattern endeared by the kabuki artist, Nakashia Shikan. Each kabuki artist had their own unique patterns.

2 Flagstone pattern in transition ⦿ CD 08_201
Laid out in a latticelike arrangement, two different types of flagstone become the base design in this bold and modern pattern.

3 Thin stripes ⦿ CD 08_202
Vertical stripes highlight the design, while brackets shaped like the Japanese character "ko" are positioned to form an argyle pattern that accentuates and strengthens the impression of the pattern.

4 Yoshihara tsunagi linked pattern ⦿ CD 08_203
A famous pattern that was used in the fireplace in Yoshihara tea shops. The slightly indented four-cornered design is distinctive.

⦿ CD 08 204 – 207

Stripes – 2

■ Patterns featuring large and small dots and rows of highly unique shapes
■ Diverse patterns that one never gets tired of looking at

Stripes constructed of familiar elements designed on the basis of unfettered concepts

The elements that comprise the stripes are diverse, and the patterns derive their charm form their rich transformations. Though not typical, these patterns that render elements of nature and the utensils of daily life as small pattern designs on kimono and furnishings enjoyed the overwhelming advocacy of the common folk of the Edo Period

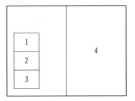

1 Stripes in transition ⦿ CD 08_204
This rendition is charming for the rhythmical nature of the continuity of the uniform dots and the pictogram-like lightness of its taste.

2 Water stripes ⦿ CD 08_205
A variety of forms of water are integrated to form two contrasting stripe patterns.

3 Arrow fletchings rendered as stripes
⦿ CD 08_206
The arrow is significant for its ability to ward off evil spirits, and being superstitious, the Japanese people have rendered the arrow in a variety of designs. Here, arrows have been arranged in equal intervals to create a design based on the fletchings.

4 Crafted stripes ⦿ CD 08_207
This pattern, comprised of diamonds and circles, is light and seemingly so comfortable that it will sweep away the summer's heat in an instant.

● CD 08 208 – 211

Stripes – 3

- ■ Original concepts unrestricted by the framework of the pattern
- ■ Taking on the new challenge of rendition as playfully and freely as possible

The round shapes dance and the curving lines undulate. Patterns given life by creativity groping for innovative expression

During the Edo Period the straightforwardness of the vertical stripe pattern enjoyed wide popularity. One may also observe patterns that have made an attempt to venture into a new world of values while remaining true to the fundamental rule of the vertical stripe. This was a period of history during which such innovations were considered stylish and sophisticated.

	4
1	
2	
3	

1 **Wavy bamboo stripes** ● CD 08_208
The leaves of the bamboo accentuate this pattern of wavelike amplitude rendered with gently curving dot shapes.

2 **Wavy stripes** ● CD 08_209
Patterns of slightly billowing shapes, referred to as "wavy," have given birth to a variety of free-wheeling designs. These patterns are not completely unrelated to the rise of the townspeople classes of the Edo Period.

3 **Broken stripes in transition** ● CD 08_210
Though at first glance it would seem that this pattern does not merit repetition, the creator has rigidly protected the integrity of his pattern. But one marvels at the degree of freedom evident in this example.

4 **Wavy stripes in transition** ● CD 08_211
Here, the movement of water has been simplified to an extreme to render this pattern. The impression of the liveliness the water communicates well.

⦿ CD 08 212 – 215

Lattice – 1

- ■ A fundamental design among textile patterns
- ■ Well-received by the common people, an attempt at solicitation that shattered the borders of the lattice pattern

A popular pattern that epitomized its era

The lattice introduced here is a design based on complex repeating patterns that are rich with Japanese beauty. These patterns, crisscrossing on a vertical and horizontal axis, are form-enriched and quite avant-garde. During the Edo Period, as the culture of the townspeople thrived, these excellent patterns began to appear with increasing frequency.

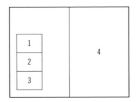

1 Iris and kuginuki pattern ⦿ CD 08_212
Here, kuginuki refers to the small square in the center of the diamond shapes rendered in this linked pattern depicting cored metal washers.

2 Lattice pattern in transition ⦿ CD 08_213
Consisting mainly of three thick vertical lines and two thick horizontal lines that encapsulate designs rendered to resemble the fletchings of an arrow, this pattern was intentionally created to seem complicated.

3 Lattice pattern in transition ⦿ CD 08_214
Broken lines are intermittently integrated with thick and thin vertical lines, attributing a sense of rhythm that rids the rendition of monotony.

4 Lattice and cranes ⦿ CD 08_215
Despite the use of thick uniform lines, this is a highly refined pattern. The form of the cranes has been rendered in a design seemingly intended to be a simplified model for the observation of nature.

● CD 08 216 – 219

Lattice – 2

■ Diagonal lines in effectively arrayed variation
■ The standard pattern elements take on a certain significance and enhance elegance

Despite their complicated appearance, the basic form of the lattice pattern supports the faithful rendition of design

The diamond-shaped lattice could be referred to as an argyle variant of the usual lattice pattern. The lines that intersect each other diagonally create a stronger effect than the straightforward vertical and horizontal lines. Modifying the shape, number, and angle of the lines that comprise the stripes enables the free expression of delicacy, strength, and other traits. In effect, the possibilities for variation are limitless.

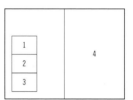

1 Matsukawa overlapping argyle patterns
● CD 08_216
At first glance, this composition seems complicated and lacking in unity, but in fact, this is a design that combines two patterns to create a strong impression.

2 A transitioning contiguous argyle pattern embedded with flowers ● CD 08_217
From this design of argyle patterns with flowers embedded in openings, one can see the well-balanced pattern area and get a sense of its stable cohesiveness.

3 Argyle pattern ● CD 08_218
In this culmination of form, the argyle cross lines, the circles, and decorative patterns come together in a well-balanced composition that unconsciously incorporates all of the composite elements of the pattern.

4 Narihira-hishi pattern ● CD 08_219
The sizes of the dots that comprise the lines are exquisitely rendered in this delicate and intellectual pattern where even the most minute details stimulate the senses

⊙ CD 08 220 – 223
Circles

■ The form of the minimal structural unit used in planer patterns
■ Elements required to establish the best layout for harmonization of a pattern

The basic element of geometric design that expresses peace and spiritual stability

For a long time circles have been integrated in patterns as designs of good fortune that signify spiritual stability and peace. Prior to the Edo Period, there were numerous examples of designs featuring circular patterns. After the Edo Period, however, arcs also came to be used as a unit of patterns in geometric design.

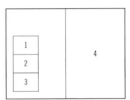

1 Contrary circles ⊙ CD 08_220
A contiguous pattern of complex linked overlapping circles, among the yusokumon patterns which were used to determine one's level or title. They were also known as "seven treasures."

2 An interlocking "seven treasures" pattern embedded with small flowers ⊙ CD 08_221
A pattern with small, five-petaled flowers randomly placed in the center of a "seven treasures" pattern. The circular shape of the "seven treasures" pattern signifies happiness and peace.

3 Interlocking circles ⊙ CD 08_222
A pattern of linked overlapping circles, this term has the same meaning as "contrary circles" in figure 1 above. This pattern further incorporates bands of stripes in a more complex fashion.

4 Circle patterns and columns of flowers ⊙ CD 08_223
As a geometrical structural element, four-petaled flowers with cross-shaped stamen are effectively distributed in this pattern.

■ **Linked hemp leaves** ◗ **CD 08_224** Owing to the hemp leaflike shapes, this hexagonal pattern containing numerous evolving forms has been named "hemp leaf." While this rendition of "hemp leaf" adheres to the basic pattern, it also boldly transforms the structural elements, creating a exceptionally liberated design.

■ **Mountain roads** ◗ **CD 08_225** Also known as "mountain path", this pattern is comprised of zigzagging lines and shapes that symbolize the roads going from mountain to mountain. This zigzagging form is used often in stripe patterns as well.

Chapter 9
Utensils/Formats

● CD 09 226 – 229
Utensils

■ Designs that arose from observing one's immediate surroundings
■ The discovery of ideas that develop and evolve through random change

The technique of observing and then simplifying the shapes of objects and sights from everyday life

Designs based on implements or tools are employed in both interior and exterior environments. The most impressive trait of this category is the way the designs are based on simplified forms of the implements so integral to the Japanese sense of everyday life. Perhaps these patterns seem so natural because they are used in clothes and furnishings that are parts of weddings and other ritual events.

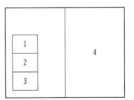

1 Komon pattern "maple leaves on the surface of fans" ● CD 09_226
Perhaps as a result of the motif of fans and maple leaves, the different dots and lines cultivate a sense of elegance.

2 Komon pattern "entwined patterns"
● CD 09_227
Created from scattered, intertwined patterns, the design expresses a loose playfulness.

3 Komon pattern "oriental pipe pattern"
● CD 09_228
The idea of basing a pattern on oriental pipes is ingenious. While this pattern lacks the rich imagery of designs based on fans and umbrellas, one can say that it compensates with novelty.

4 Spool ● CD 09_229
With sprawling threads and spools as accents, this design inspires the viewer and hints at new designs.

● CD 09 230 – 233
Tortoise Shell – 1

- Highly valued as a design that represents good omens
- A fundamental, infinitely repeating pattern

A sense of joyous creativity that has escaped fixed patterns and grown into a crest

Since the Heian Period, the association with good omens has made the tortoise shell design one of the Yusoku Monyo, a group of designs used in official buildings and ceremonious settings. Designs composed of tiled or repeating tortoise shell designs are called "kameko tsunagi" (linked tortoise shells), and designs composed of tortoise shells containing flower patterns are called "kameko hanamon" (tortoise shell flower patterns). People in those days had an amazing artistic sensibility, and we can all learn from their joyous sense of creativity.

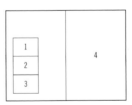

1 Komon pattern "hanagatsumi in tortoise shell"
● CD 09_230
When one thinks of tortoise shell patterns, one usually thinks of fixed patterns. However, one could also call this lovely tortoise shell a kind of flower pattern.

2 Komon pattern "embedded pattern linked tortoise shells" ● CD 09_231
A design of patterns within patterns, this design provides an example of using the tortoise shell pattern's order while allowing the motif to make a statement from within.

3 Komon pattern "linked tortoise shells"
● CD 09_232
Though a simple design, we can learn a great deal from the fact that the illusion of depth is created so easily.

4 Komon pattern "embedded pattern linked tortoise shells" ● CD 09_233
By encapsulating and overlaying komon, this design becomes complex and gorgeous without seeming chaotic because the order imposed by the tortoise shell lattice never breaks down.

● CD 09 234 – 237

Tortoise Shell – 2

■ An independent motif for which there should be a separate name
■ A fundamental, infinitely repeating pattern

A new fixed pattern motif, the evolution of the tortoise shell into pure design

Bishamon kameko is an evolved form of the tortoise shell pattern. Made from units of three tortoise shells arranged together, this pattern is named after the pattern on the armor of Bishamonten. The virtue of this variation on the tortoise shell motif is that it allows the pattern to be infinite for whatever range of space on which it is rendered.

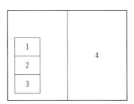

1 Komon pattern "bishamon-linked tortoise shells"
● CD 09_234
With points that have a softer feeling than the conventional tortoise shell motif, this pattern is suitable for garments.

2 Komon pattern "bishamon-linked tortoise shells"
● CD 09_235
It is easy to see that even when using the same materials the results can vary depending on the expression.

3 Komon pattern "obi tortoise shell"
● CD 09_236
A unique and modern variation on the primary form, this design also allows for an infinitely extendable pattern.

4 Komon pattern "embedded pattern bishamon-linked tortoise shells" ● CD 09_237
Like number 4 on page 132, "embedded pattern linked tortoise shells," this design is both complex and gorgeous.

⦿ CD 09 238 – 241
Tachiwaku

■ Continuing patterns that use twin curves to portray concave and convex surfaces
■ A standard design that widely uses themes like chrysanthemums, bamboo grass, and clouds

A pattern that suggests steam twisting and rising in symmetry

The impetus to create a design from the undulation one finds in the natural world reveals a great deal about the distinctive artistic sensibility of the Japanese. A fundamental supporting element of Japanese design, this motif's widespread visibility in varied settings is testament to the strength of its symbolism and the softness of its characteristic curves.

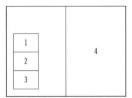

❶ Komon pattern "tachiwaku and fans"
⦿ CD 09_238
A creative variation which breaks out of the category of Yusoku Monyo by tracing the curved edges of the fans.

❷ Komon pattern "rain dragon tachiwaku on seigaiha" ⦿ CD 09_239
Even the tachiwaku contains a pattern. The seigaiha pattern—created by overlaying concentric circles and half-circles—is used as a design over a broad range; surely the design was intended to leverage the resulting contrast.

❸ Komon pattern "tachiwaku with bamboo joints"
⦿ CD 09_240
Depending on what is placed inside the bulges of the tachiwaku, we have names like "chrysanthemum tachiwaku," "paulownia tachiwaku," and "cloud tachiwaku," so this pattern should be "bamboo tachiwaku." This design communicates the humor of the artist well.

❹ Komon pattern "tachiwaku with cherry blossom pattern" ⦿ CD 09_241
By reducing the cherry blossoms to symbols and using the white tachiwaku line to make it a repeating pattern, the impact of the design itself is strengthened.

⦿ CD 09 242 – 245
Characters

■ A pattern that concretely communicates a message
■ Character patterns that combine connotations of good omens with an inherent aesthetic value

A clear and precise pattern that directly links the originator to the recipient of the image

One might consider these designs as representations of a particular message. For example, a woman wearing a lovely, unspoiled flower crest perhaps chose that design as a signal to express to the viewer her interests and the image she wants to convey. If patterns are conceived of in this way, then character patterns can be thought of as attempts to more clearly and definitely communicate what could be the vague "signal" of a noncharacter pattern.

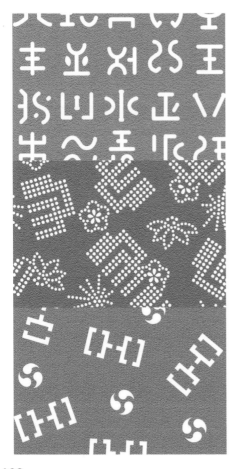

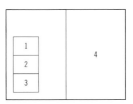

1 Komon pattern "stylized good fortune characters" ⦿ CD 09_242
Most commonly used good fortune characters are "long life/ kotobuki," "prosperity/ fuku," and "luck/ kichi." In this crest, the characters are stylized, so looking at them one still gets an idea that they are somewhat associated with good fortune.

2 Komon pattern "genjiko and pine, bamboo, and plum" ⦿ CD 09_243
Genjikou is a game in which five rectangular sticks of incense are used in distinguishing between the incense.

3 Komon pattern "three variations of ryo" ⦿ CD 09_244
Perhaps this is an attempt to infuse the sixth tone of ancient Japanese Gagaku court music and the number three with meaning. An interesting design.

4 Hanten character ⦿ CD 09_245
These patterns seem to have been useful in fostering group pride by illustrating the superior, inferior, and peer relationships between organizations of the same type and profession.

⏺ CD 09 246 – 249
Yusoku

■ Garment crests used in the Imperial Court that were regulated by court rank
■ Pinnacles of artistic beauty that should be maintained

Designs unparalleled in well-ordered and dignified beauty

In the Heian Era, these patterns were restricted by social class and tradition (clothing, officials, rank, age, etc.), so it was not possible to use them freely for clothing and furnishings. These patterns are without equal for the beauty of their well-ordered and dignified designs. As time has passed, these patterns have lost their beauty, but they have come to be comparatively freely modified and altered.

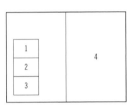

1 **Whirlpools on embroidered foil-cloth**
⏺ CD 09_246
Because this pattern was used in the "Kanzesui Ryu" of Noh, it came to be known as "Nuihaku no Kanzesui." It seems that a noble classic pattern was employed as a Yusoku Monyo.

2 **Komon pattern "tortoise shell flower argyle pattern"** ⏺ CD 09_247
Four argyle shapes, each containing flower petals arranged in an argyle formation is another of the Yusoku Monyo. This pattern, with the flower argyle pattern within the celebratory tortoise shell pattern carries strong connotations of the Heian Period.

3 **Komon pattern "cloud tachiwaku pattern"**
⏺ CD 09_248
It is hard to find a pattern that has been transformed into an icon to the extent of the cloud tachiwaku pattern. One reason might be because it is so modern.

4 **Peony arabesque rendered on a twill short-sleeved kimono** ⏺ CD 09_249
A famous rendition of this same pattern is known as the "crab peony/ kani botan", because the peony, being woven in red, looks like a crab.

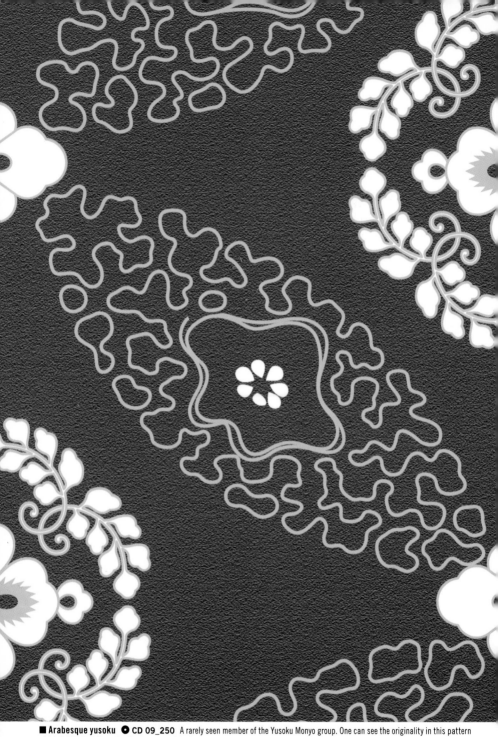

■ **Arabesque yusoku** ◉ **CD 09_250** A rarely seen member of the Yusoku Monyo group. One can see the originality in this pattern which faithfully follows the fixed pattern of the "seven treasures."

[About the Author]

Shigeki Nakamura An art director since 1964, he established Cobble Corporation Co. Ltd. in 1987. The company published a book of ESP Pattern Library Digital Materials, which can be seen on its website (http://www.cobbleart.com/). He has received many awards, such as the Minister of International Trade and Industry Award, and he is a member of the JAGDA (Japanese Graphic Designer Association).